The Long Road Home
Helen's Journey with Alzheimer's

by

Brenda Springhetti

PITTSBURGH, PENNSYLVANIA 15222

RoseDog Books
701 Smithfield Street
Pittsburgh, PA 15222
Visit our website at *www.rosedogbookstore.com*

ISBN: 978-1-4349-8817-1
eISBN: 978-1-4349-7811-0

THE EARLY STAGE

Denial

Looking back it's hard to pinpoint exactly when our family knew that something was wrong with Mom. There had been little signs along the way that we subconsciously dismissed. "Well, she just got a little confused," we'd explain or "Hey, everyone forgets a word now and then." No big deal. Of course we were more than willing to find reasons to dismiss our concerns. Denial is a powerful defense mechanism. It's preferable to just let things slide awhile, as opposed to facing the reality of a loved one facing a life changing health situation such as Alzheimer's.

I, of all people in my family, should have recognized not only Mom's symptoms, but my own reluctance to acknowledge them for what they were. I had been recently hired as a recreation assistant at Project Independence, an adult day care that was run by Goodwill Industries of Southeast Wisconsin. Participants that I had daily contact with included people who were in the early to mid stages of Alzheimer's. I also observed first-hand how family members sometimes were caught in the clutches of the Denial Monster.

I remember approaching my supervisor early on and expressing some of my concerns after a recent visit with Mom. I relayed this incident to her.

We were all sitting around after dinner and Mom was getting ready to serve dessert. She said "Well, why don't I bring over the....the... (she paused) you know...the thing that you bake with the brown stuff spread on it."
"Cake?" my sister, Lori, provided.
"That's it!" Mom said with a laugh and a shake of her head.
" Is that normal, Julie?" I asked.
She looked at me directly and with sadness said, "No, that doesn't sound right."

That was definitely NOT what I wanted to hear. Well, Julie hadn't been there and couldn't see that Mom seemed alright the rest of the weekend of my visit home. After all, that incident was one small lapse. Just let it go, let it go.

Of course the problem didn't go away. I noticed Mom struggling more and more with her speech, especially during our phone conversations. I was born and raised in the Kalamazoo, Michigan area. Since my marriage and subsequent move to Sheboygan WI, my husband, Ray, and I have always made a point of calling his parents (in Hurley, Wisconsin) and mine every Sunday to chat and catch up on the week's news. We both come from close families and our weekly conversations have kept us connected even though we can't see each other as often as we'd like.

Anyway, after my dad's death in 1991, we continued our phone conversations with Mom alone. I would even often call her myself mid-week to chat—just the two of us. Besides talking about the normal things like the grandkids and weather, we loved talking politics. We both followed the news closely and were political junkies, sharing our conservative thoughts and values. However, as time went on, it became apparent that our lively conversations were becoming harder and harder for Mom. Sometimes she seemed distracted, as if she wasn't following what I was saying. I noticed longer stretches of silence. "Mom, are you still there?" I'd ask.
"Oh yes, I'm here," she'd respond. Then the conversation would resume for awhile until the next lapse.

There were other disquieting incidences, that alone weren't worthy of concern, but cumulatively added up. Like the time Mom mistook the car's gas pedal for the brake and drove it through her garage door. (The details of this story will be saved for another chapter). Or like the times I observed her struggling with people's names. This was especially evident at the reception of her wedding to her second husband, Beryl Geren, as she tried to make introductions. She would pause and stumble until someone would rescue her, offering the correct name. It was laughed off by all as a "bride's nervousness".

Mom loved playing various board and card games. We began to notice that she was having some difficulty playing these games, to where she even started turning away from them. "I think I'll just watch a little T.V. tonight, instead," she'd say.

And then there was her famous blueberry crisp. Mom prepared this for our family every time we came home for a visit. It was her specialty; made from Michigan-grown blueberries and our family's favorite dessert. My daughter, Angie, was given a sample taste before dinner. She came up to me and whispered "Mom, there's something wrong with Grandma's blueberry crisp." She was right. This dish that my mother had prepared countless times, without even using a recipe, didn't taste right. The normally crispy topping was mushy and the blueberry filling more tart than usual. Well, after all, grandma was so busy getting ready for our visit that a mistake was perfectly understandable. She was probably in a hurry and just forgot the proportion of ingredients. See how denial takes over all sense of logic?

The most insidious aspect of denial is that the person most in need of support and comfort isn't getting it from the family that is working overtime to avoid the reality. Looking in retrospect, I'm sure Mom knew something was wrong and it scared her. I remember another visit home when Mom and I were pushing a grocery cart back to our car in the Thrifty Acres parking lot. For whatever reason, she took that opportunity of us being alone to express her concerns.

"It was good to get out and walk around the store," she said. "You know, Bren," she began hesitantly, "sometimes when I'm out taking my walk in our neighborhood, I look up at the street signs and don't recognize what I'm reading."
"What do you mean?" I asked for clarification.
"Well, I can't really explain it. I look at the signs and I get confused that they don't register with me."
"Are you saying you don't know where you are? Do you get lost?"
"No, it's not that. I always find my way home. It's just so strange that I don't recognize those signs." she trailed off.
The look in her eyes begged the question "What should I do?" I stared at her feeling totally helpless to respond.

Role Reversal

That moment marked the beginning of a change in our relationship. Here was my strong mother, whom I had always leaned on for answers, now looking to me for help. Suddenly memories of Mom giving me help and encouragement all my life flooded me. One particular incident stands out.

I was about fifteen and still going through that ugly duckling stage that most adolescents were beginning to move out of by then. But not me. I was still skinny, shy and awkward, had braces on my buck teeth, and hair that was always in a "bad hair day" mode. We had just returned from a Sunday visit with my mom's family in Elkhart, Indiana. My grandma had prepared one of her famous fried chicken dinners for all her kids and grandkids. (The whole family frequently enjoyed feasting on Grandma Boyer's Sunday dinners!) Several of my cousins who were close in age to me were there. Our ages were the *only* thing that was similar about us, since they were cute and all had boyfriends that they brought to the dinner. The closest thing I had to a boyfriend was a crush I had on the lead singer of Herman's Hermits! Actually,

I was too shy to even talk to a boy. Nevertheless, I felt bad that I didn't have a trophy boyfriend. I was feeling like an out-of-place loser around my attractive cousins and their equally attractive boyfriends. When we returned home, Mom must have sensed my sadness and asked me if anything was wrong.
"Everyone has a boyfriend, but me! What's wrong with me?" I cried.
"There's nothing wrong with you."
"Why can't I get a boy to like me?"

Mom looked deep into my eyes and gently asked, "Do you want me to tell you how? Come sit here by me on the couch." She put her arm around my shoulder and proceeded to tell me that my time would come. She told me that I had to try to overcome my shyness and initiate conversations with the other gender.
"I thought the boys were supposed to pursue!" I was astonished.
"No. Sometimes the girl has to break the ice and talk first."
"What should I say?"

Mom and I spent many close minutes together as she answered all of my tearful questions. I decided to put her advice into action. I'm sure there were many taken aback young men who didn't know what to think of the new friendly Brenda Geiger who appeared at school the next day. Brenda, who previously hadn't said boo to them in class, was now peppering them with all kinds of questions such as "What did you think of that test?" Or "Did you get your homework done?" Although the boys answered my questions and were friendly enough, no romance ensued. (After all, I still had a ways to go to move through the ugly duckling stage and that was definitely holding me back!) Regardless of the lack of success in following her advice, I will always remember Mom's sweet concern and the tender moments we spent together as she tried to help me through a bad time.

Now Mom was looking into my eyes with that same unspoken question "What's wrong with me?" I knew in that instant that the pretense had to stop. Our roles had reversed. For the first time in our lives, she was looking to *me* for advice and I couldn't let her down.

"Mom, I can see this is really bothering you. So, I think you should call and make an appointment with your doctor. Just tell him what all your concerns are and let him take it from there. I'm sure everything is alright (still some denial there) but I think it will make you feel better just finding out what's going on."

Mom seemed relieved that she had finally unburdened her fears to me and that I had not sloughed them off. Facing the hard truth is always easier if you're not facing it alone.

This actually was not the first time I had an inkling that our adult-child roles were to be reversed. In looking back, I recall a few months prior to that in June of 1999 when Mom had come to Sheboygan to help me prepare a large array of food. I was planning an open house celebrating my oldest son, Mike's, graduation from high school. Mom was eager to help out in any way she could. Mom was always a take-charge kind of person. Whenever there was a large meal to prepare she would direct my sister and me to our duties, totally taking control. This time, though, Mom seemed confused about what to do. As we readied ourselves to work in my kitchen, she stood looking at me blankly, until *I* directed *her*, giving her specific, simple directions. "Mom, why don't you take this celery that I've washed and cut it up like this." I then demonstrated with one celery rib, showing how to cut it.

"Oh, yes. I can do that," she said. She then proceeded to cut it very carefully and meticulously just as I had shown her. When she was finished with that task, I directed her to another. Quite a change from what I was accustomed to! Although I can't recall a specific conversation, it's most likely that she had dropped hints at that time about her growing concerns.

Diagnosis—Just Don't Say the "A" Word

Since I have decided to sit at this computer to capture my family's experiences during this battle with Alzheimer's, I am developing a growing regret that I did not keep a journal. It would be so convenient to be able to go back and check dates and events as they actually occurred. However, since I didn't, I must rely on my own memory (or that of my family) to come up with reasonably accurate time lines:

Aug. 1998	Beryl and Mom's wedding (difficulty with introductions)
June 1999	Mike's graduation. Confusion, memory problems surface
Later that summer	Mom expressed her concerns to me about street signs
Late in 1999	First battery of tests taken
Spring 2000	Diagnosis made

The symptoms came on so gradually that it's likely there were other troubling examples before 1998 that we don't even recall. One thing I do know for certain. By the time we finally heard the diagnosis of "Alzheimer's", it was only a confirmation of what most of us had already come to realize. I say most of us, because Beryl clung on to the hope that Mom was still alright. After all, he had recently married his Helen (also a second marriage) and all the plans and dreams of their future together were being threatened. He challenged concerns expressed by others about her speech and memory problems.

"When everyone worries about her so much, it just makes Helen nervous," he chided. "No wonder she gets confused. She just needs to learn to relax."

In fact, "relax" was essentially the initial advice given by a medical professional. Shortly after our discussion in the parking lot, Mom did see her family doctor, who then referred her to a psychologist. She underwent a battery of tests that measured memory, comprehension, etc. She called me to excitedly relay the results.

"I've been told that there is nothing "conclusively" wrong. I'm to go on living my life and not worry so much. I feel so relieved." I rejoiced with her at the news and we all were given a little more time of false hope.

Mom's symptoms, of course, only grew worse, causing her to seek more medical advice. Whenever a doctor would mention the possibility of Alzheimer's being the root of her problems, she would abruptly switch doctors. She absolutely refused to listen to the "A" word. Mom hung onto her own denial as long as she could.

Eventually the inevitable diagnosis was made by a neurologist. Several months later, after undergoing yet another battery of tests, the doctor called Mom, Beryl, Lori, and me into her office for the results. We listened as it was explained that the possibility that Mom was experiencing small strokes or any other physical problem had all been ruled out. That left the conclusion that Mom was suffering from early stages of Alzheimer's.

I looked at Mom to gauge her reaction. A few months previous to this, hearing the word "Alzheimer's" would have been devastating to her. (Ironically, Mom had often expressed the hope that as she aged she wouldn't "lose her mind" in some way). But that day Mom didn't bat an eye. She just kept nodding politely as the doctor continued to explain what we could all expect in the near and distant future. She also prescribed medication to help in slowing down the progression of the disease. Possible side effects were discussed.

Of course we all had questions that were patiently answered by the doctor. There were some questions that just could not be answered. Like "How did she get this?" I had heard there could be a hereditary link, and that made no sense to me since no one in my mom's extended family had ever experienced this. In fact, my grandma and great-grandma both lived well into their nineties and were mentally sharp until theirs deaths. Mom was only sixty nine! And as far as mental acuity, Mom had always been sharp herself. She had worked in an insurance office handling complicated claims, for goodness sake. And how many people have learned to play a difficult game like Bridge (and played it so well) as she did? How could this be? I felt outraged that my mother should be so cheated at this relatively young age!

During the course of our conversation, Mom remained quiet. The doctor asked her if she understood everything that had been explained. Mom nodded and said "yes." Dr. Lang then followed up, "Do *you* have any questions?" Mom shook her head and replied "no." It wasn't until we were alone outside the doctor's office that we asked Mom her reaction to the diagnosis.
"So, what do you think of all this?"
She looked at us quizzically and asked "Is this something bad?"

It seemed as though the ramifications of this diagnosis had gone totally over her head. Maybe that was a blessing for her sake. Lori and I just looked at each other and didn't know how to respond. But Beryl's dry sense of humor kicked in as he quipped, "Well, it sure isn't good!" The information provided by the doctor had finally led to Beryl's acceptance of Mom's condition.

Early Intervention

As it turned out, the meeting Beryl, Lori, and I had with Mom's doctor was the first of many such meetings with various doctors, home health care professionals, hospice workers etc. Not to mention the countless conversations between the three of us as we navigated our way through coping with this disease step by step. As new situations arose, new decisions were made all in Mom's behalf. We tried to be as open as possible, including Mom in most discussions. None of us wanted to appear to be "going behind her back" although there were some instances when we really needed to talk privately. During these family talks Mom would typically sit quietly and listen, contributing only a "yes" or "no" when asked a question.

The relationship my sister and I had with Beryl grew slowly over the next several months. At first things were a little awkward. Since Beryl was not our father, we felt we could not be quite as blunt as we would have liked at times. Complicating the issue was Beryl's initial resentment of Lori and I having sole power of attorney over Mom's health and finances (even though this was Mom's decision—not ours). Second marriages later in life can produce financial complications, and Mom and Beryl's marriage was no exception. Prior to marrying Beryl, Mom had insisted that their finances be kept separate. And that any final decisions regarding her health or finances would be left to Lori and me if she became incapacitated. Beryl once commented: "You girls could just put Helen away into a nursing home without me having anything to say about it."
Yes, we could have. But we assured him over and over we would never do anything without his input.

I later came to realize that Beryl probably was also worried about what would become of *him* if Mom, indeed, was ever placed in a nursing home. (After they were married, Mom and Beryl came to live in *her* house that Beryl had no legal claim to. I suppose in the back of Beryl's mind was the fear that Lori and I could "throw him out" whenever it suited us). Once we were able to reassure him that Mom's house was for him to live in for as long as he liked, he seemed to relax and the situation eased.

We continued to talk openly to Beryl seeking his opinion on all decisions. Slowly, he came to trust us. And as Lori and I got to know him better, we came to appreciate his sense of humor and his true love and concern for Mom's well being. Our husbands, Ray and Paul, were also called upon for advice. Together, we developed into a strong united team. Although there were some minor disagreements along the way about various issues, in the end, we always came to a consensus.

Throughout the years that followed Lori and I came to look upon Beryl, not as a father substitute, not as just Mom's husband, but as another family member who we came to love. When he had hip surgery I stayed with him a few days to help out after he returned home to recuperate. Lori and Paul lent aid by occasionally accompanying him to doctor's appointments or fixing something at the house that needed repair. They often had him over for dinner and checked on him periodically. I think it's noteworthy to mention here, that several years later when Beryl lay dying in a hospital, he asked his own children to call Lori and Paul so that they could be by his side as well.

******

One of the first decisions our family had to make was easy for us, but heartbreaking for my mom. Per her doctor's strong recommendation, it was determined that Mom should no longer get behind a steering wheel.

"I can still drive!" she emphatically insisted.

We told Mom that her lack of judgment made it dangerous for her to be on the road. Our explanations did not sit well with her. "That's silly! I'm perfectly capable of driving!"

To prove it, one morning a few days later, she hopped into her car and drove down the street to my sister's house, after she had witnessed Lori and Paul drive away. My niece, Emily, was home alone and when she told her grandma that her parents had just left on an errand, Mom feigned innocence. "Oh, that's too bad," she said coyly. "Well, at least I can visit you." Then she grinned broadly at Emily. "See, I told you I can still drive," she crowed triumphantly.

Fortunately, Lori only lived a few houses from hers and Mom didn't have to travel on any busy road to get there. After that incident, Mom's car keys mysteriously disappeared and that was the last time she ever drove.

Mom's car represented her freedom. Freedom to go wherever and whenever she wanted. Losing that independence was a huge blow to her. Eventually, she came to accept that she would no longer be driving. Getting rid of her beloved car, however, was another matter.

We let Mom's car sit in the garage for several months before we approached her about selling it. This was another hurdle. We explained that Beryl could take her wherever she wanted to go in his car. Ray and I were interested in purchasing her Buick at the "blue book" price to be used as an extra family car. Mom would have none of this. "I was thinking of saving this for Emily or Andy (my sister's children) to use when they'll need an extra car." I think Mom figured that if she couldn't drive it, at the very least she wanted the car to stay within close proximity. That way she would still be able to see it every day. After all, my mom bought that car herself after my dad died. She went to the dealer, negotiated the price, and took full ownership of it. There's no way she wanted it to end up as far away as Sheboygan. Unfortunately for her, my niece and nephew had no interest in an old-folks type of car. They had their own ideas that didn't include Mom's old model. (By the way, that car is still running today!)

"Mom, we will take very good care of your car. And every time you come to visit us in Sheboygan we'll take you for rides in it," we promised.

Eventually, she did relent and we purchased the car. True to our word, we drove her around in it whenever she came to visit. Mom eventually forgot that she had ever owned it, but at the time, giving up her car was a tremendous loss. Unbeknownst to her, this was only the first of many losses she was to experience on this long Alzheimer's road.

Adult Day Care

The second crucial decision we made in this early stage was finding an adult day care center for Mom to attend several days a week. As mentioned previously, I was working in an adult day care facility myself, so I was aware of the importance of this kind of early intervention. Providing stimulating activities and community outings to the Alzheimer's patient promotes socialization and feelings of self worth. As the disease progresses, it is perhaps even more crucial that the main caregiver be given a break from the day to day frustrations that are inevitable. Adult day care provides the caregiver that opportunity to have some time to him or herself. That benefit can not be understated.

One of the biggest mistakes families make is to wait too long before seeking refuge. Caregivers tend to feel it is their responsibility to care for loved ones. By the time it's realized that the load is just too heavy to handle alone, it may be too late for the Alzheimer's patient to adjust. Regardless of when the day care experience begins, there is usually some resistance by the participant. But the longer one waits, the stronger the resistance becomes. I experienced that with some of our potential participants who absolutely refused to even try to cooperate in our program. Staff members had to literally stand guard at the door to prevent an angry, defiant person from leaving. After several days of making every attempt to help the participant to adapt (without success), it was eventually realized that the situation was impossible. The participant's family was informed that, regretfully, other arrangements would have to be made.

Initially, I sensed reluctance from Beryl and Lori to enroll Mom in adult day care. After all, this was an admission that our family was incapable of handling this problem. In the long run, relinquishing total control is the kindest act one can do. A successful adjustment to adult day care usually allows the Alzheimer's patient to remain in the home longer than if a family tries to "go it alone".

Eventually, Beryl and Lori came to accept my point of view, and arrangements were made. We were fortunate to find a center that was located in a church only a few miles from Mom's home. Lori, Beryl, and I visited the day care and we were duly impressed. It was a clean facility run by compassionate staff and volunteers. The participants seemed quietly content as they were in engaged in various activities. We were satisfied. Now we just had to convince Mom.

Mom was already losing the ability to reason and display sound judgment. This was a change from the take-charge Mom I had always known and admired. After Dad died in 1991, I was proud of Mom's strength of character and acceptance of just what she needed to do in her life changing situation. She was not one to sit around feeling sorry for herself. Instead, she demonstrated a strong independent spirit and the courage to adapt to situations as they warranted. The first time she drove around Chicago by herself to visit us in Wisconsin, I think I was more worried than she was. I expressed relief when she arrived, but Mom just shrugged it off. "There was nothing to it. I stayed in the center lane all the way from Michigan and just kept going with the flow of traffic." To always "go with the flow" seemed to be Mom's unspoken philosophy of life.

Besides dealing with getting her finances in order, Mom also seemed to recognize the importance of remaining active in the community once she was on her own. Without any encouragement from anyone, she joined the Portage Senior Center and a Widow/Widower's group. This was where she met (and eventually married) Beryl. Now, at this point in Mom's life, it was even more important that she not become isolated in her home. However, trying to explain this to her proved difficult. Our conversation went something like this:

"Mom, we think it would be very good for you to attend this adult day care center close to your home. You'll meet other people your age who will become new friends and there are lots of interesting activities to participate in."
"Can Beryl come with me?" she asked.
"No, he'll stay at home. Beryl and you do a lot of things together. But sometimes it's good for both of you to have time to yourselves. Beryl has things he likes to do, and you can explore new interests with your friends at the day care. It's only for a few hours a day. Then when you come home, you and Beryl can still do those things that you share together. So what do you think?"
"I guess that will be o.k. But why can't Beryl come with me?"
And around it went.

Mom was already becoming dependent on Beryl. At this early phase of Alzheimer's, she was still aware that she had problems with memory, comprehension, and speech. New situations without someone familiar at her side frightened her. Although we gave her repeated reassurances that the people who ran the day care would be able to help her in any way she needed, she was still, understandably, afraid.

So, Mom began attending the day care with the resistance I had expected. Every morning that she was to attend she would look at Beryl and ask "Why can't you come too?" Before I left to go back to Wisconsin, I reminded Beryl that he must remain firm and not allow Mom to talk him out of taking her. I know this was very hard for Beryl, but he complied. Eventually, Mom's resistance subsided, and her time spent at day care became a part of her routine.

At this point, I want to revisit the whole area of role reversal that Lori and I both had to go through in our own time. For my sister, I think Mom's attendance in adult day care was like a douse of cold reality thrown into her face.

Lori's situation was quite different from mine. While I had moved out-of-state in my early twenties, Lori has remained in Portage her whole life. In fact, shortly after their marriage, Paul and Lori bought my parents home. (My parents moved up the street to live with my Grandpa Geiger who had been alone since my grandma's passing.) Living so close, Lori and Mom shared a very special mother-daughter relationship. They frequently talked on the phone, went for coffee together, stopped by each other's house etc. Hardly a day went by when they weren't in contact with each other in some way. Later, when Lori had children, Mom was a built-in babysitter (and dog sitter, as well). Mom participated fully in her grandchildren's lives, attending school functions and sporting events. When Emily or Andy became sick, Lori asked Mom for advice and she would either give instructions or else come right over in person. Lori could always count on her to be there when needed. At times, I felt very envious of that!

But now here was Mom, the one Lori had always relied on, attending an activity program much like the early childhood programs that Mom's grandchildren had once attended. I can remember a time when Lori called me after visiting her at the day care. She choked back tears as she exclaimed "My mother has been reduced to making kindergarten crafts!" Kindergarten crafts that were proudly displayed on the refrigerator and on countertops, as her grandchildren's work had once been displayed.

I'm not sure exactly when Lori came to an acceptance of the role reversal that we both experienced, but accept it she did. Later, I will go into detail about all that my sister has done for my mom on this long road. For now, suffice it to say that Lori became Mom's greatest support and advocate for her well being. She has truly "mothered" our mother as only a loving daughter could do.

Brenda with her parents

Ken and Helen Geiger

Ken, Helen, Brenda, and Lori Geiger

Helen with Her Grandchildren

Angie and Mike

Dan

Having fun with Mike

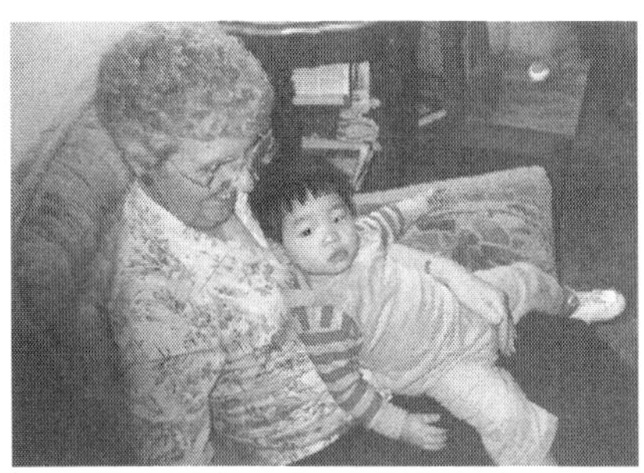

Andy

Emily and Grand-doggie, Fergie

Ken and Helen Sharing a Meal with Paul, Lori, and Emily

Celebrating Ken and Helen's 40th Wedding Anniversary

Helen Loved to Drive!

THE FEISTY STAGE

As time went on and Alzheimer's progressed, Mom entered what I call the "feisty" stage of her disease. At this point our family began noticing behavioral changes that weren't typical of her personality.

Although Mom was a strong, independent woman who wasn't afraid to speak her mind, there was also a soft gentleness about her. She exuded a calm spirit, rarely getting riled up about anything. Not that she wouldn't stand up for herself (or her children) if the need arose. She certainly proved she had the spunk to do that, as I will soon give a few examples of. So that feistiness was always there, under the surface, just waiting to burst into flames. Alzheimer's was the spark that ignited it.

A Little History

Mom was born Helen Nadine Boyer in Salem Missouri on October 21, 1931. She was the fifth of six children. I suppose that being one of the youngest and surrounded by four brothers was good training for strong, emotional toughness! Her parents, Otis and Effie, eventually moved the family to Elkhart, Indiana where much of the family still resides today.

Mom never talked much about her childhood, but by the few accounts that she did share, it was a happy one. The Boyers have always been a close-knit family. After Mom's marriage to my dad, Kenneth Geiger, the couple moved to Portage, MI. Lori and I came on the scene soon after and they began raising a family there. Since Portage was only an hour's drive from Elkhart, our family made many weekend trips to visit all the Boyers.

Growing up with just one sister, it was always fun to get together with the extended family of aunts, uncles, and cousins. I have so many fond memories of fun times shared with my cousins during our visits. Memories like walking to the mom and pop store to buy candy, exploring a near-by old deserted house that we considered "haunted", running to Grandpa for pocket change whenever we heard music from an approaching ice cream truck, eating Grandma's delicious meals that she made from scratch without a recipe, and playing outdoor games and catching lightning bugs well into the twilight. Then, at the end of the day, piling into Grandma's feather mattress that she pulled out onto the floor for a night of ghost stories and giggling with my cousins. Those were happy times.

While we kids played, Mom would enjoy visiting with her family. As previously mentioned, she was always close with her brothers and sister. The memories that are formed early must remain deep and safe, long after others are forgotten. Later, when Alzheimer's had really taken it's toll, (and it was often hard for me to get any reaction from her), I was surprised at how excited Mom became whenever her siblings came to visit her at the assisted living center. She would rush up to them as they entered the door, seeming to recognize them. At that point I wasn't at all sure if she remembered who *I* was. But she was so happy and excited to greet the family she remembered from her childhood.

I recall an incident about this time was when my Aunt Lil came to visit Mom. She was still in bed from her afternoon nap. Lori and I were in the room when my aunt arrived. She took Mom's hand, and said "Hi there, Howa Deenie." (Howa Deenie was a nickname my Uncle Ralph had given Mom when he was small. He couldn't pronounce Helen Nadine, so it came out Howa Deenie. The name stuck. As did my aunt's nickname, Itily May, for Lily May.) Anyway, none of us expected Mom to respond to her nickname since she rarely spoke at that point. To our surprise, she looked directly at her sister and very softly, but distinctly, whispered "Itily May".

Mom loved to laugh and tease with loved ones. I imagine that as a child she had a playful spirit that she definitely kept with her into adulthood. She had a most distinctive laugh that was heard often. I remember so many incidents of Mom playfully teasing my kids, especially my youngest son, Dan. He was really a little imp and liked to instigate trouble. Mom would have none of him getting the best of her. She would chase him around the house, laughing and saying "I'm going to scutch you!" Then when she caught him she would give him playful spanks (or sometimes tickles) to let him know that she won that round—laughing all the while.

Mom held on to that playful, feisty spirit even when she was in assisted living. The workers would tell Lori and me of her frequent laughing fits. Her face would light up and she would break into shoulder shaking laughter for one reason or another. One aide related a familiar sounding incident to us. This aid was a tall young man. He told us that when he first came to care for Mom, whenever he would turn his back on her, she would "scutch" him on the butt. He would quickly turn around to face her and she would be convulsed in laughter, much like she had been with Dan. By this time Mom had lost most of her ability to speak, but she could still laugh! The workers there fondly referred to her as their laughing "grandma".

There are many examples of Mom's fun-loving laughter. Like the time from my childhood when she taught her neighbor and best friend to ride a bike. We *all* laughed as we watched Mom run alongside Geri's wobbly bicycle, encouraging her to "balance".

Mom's feisty spirit sometimes took on a less playful note when she needed to defend herself or her family. One such incident occurred shortly after her marriage when she had taken an office job in a small company. One of her duties was to sort the daily mail. Another worker brought in that mail every morning and would dump it on top of all the other papers on her desk, mixing them all together. After several times of nicely asking this person to please put the mail carefully to the side, only to be deliberately ignored, Mom had finally had enough. She warned the worker that if she dumped the mail rudely like that again, she would regret it. The next morning, after the nemesis looked Mom in the eye and ceremoniously dumped it once again on top of her papers, Mom made good on her warning. She punched her! After that, Mom never had problems with that co-worker again. And, instead of being fired as one might assume, she was promoted to another job. My dad liked to relate that story to family and friends. Whether or not it was embellished is not known. Regardless, one of our close family friends was so amused by the story that he gave Mom the nickname "Slugger".

Another time that Mom shed her normally sweet disposition to show her feistier side, was for my sake. I was a teenager and we had been shopping together for a dress in one of those shops that cater to petite teens. I had found the dress that I really wanted, but the only one in my size was on a display mannequin. When I asked the sales clerk if I could try it on I was refused, the reason being that it was the display.

"What do you mean?" Mom asked flabbergasted. "We want to purchase that dress, but there are none in Brenda's size on the rack. The only one available is on the display."

"Sorry, I can't take it off the model," was the response.

The exchange went back and forth until the snotty sales clerk eventually turned around and walked back to the sales desk.

"Well! Maybe you can't, but I sure can!" Mom said to no one in particular.

She then strode purposefully to the model and, to my embarrassment, began pulling pins out left and right until she had removed the dress from the plastic life-sized Barbie. Then she marched up to the desk and announced "We'll take this one!"

I trailed behind Mom as the sales clerk backed down and, without another word, rang up the sale. I glanced over my shoulder to see if anyone else had witnessed the episode, dying of humiliation at the scene Mom had created. But then I thought "What the heck?" As we both walked out of the boutique, heads held high, we were triumphant in the knowledge that: *We Got the Dress!!*

Feisty, Fun, and Frustrating Times

I hope from the previous examples, the reader draws the correct conclusion of Mom's basic temperament; that of a sweet, loving person whose feisty behavior occasionally manifested itself when situations warranted. Our family was about to experience that feisty side of Mom more and more in the coming months.

This behavior first began to show up as small acts of defiance and demands. Lori recalls how Mom would come sneaking down the street to her house with insurance and financial papers that had come in the mail, secretly tucked into her jacket. "I want to keep these papers somewhere safe at your house, where Beryl can't see them," she said conspiratorially.

We were so puzzled by this paranoid action. Beryl would be the *last* person to try to take advantage of her by gaining knowledge of her finances. As was mentioned previously, Beryl and Mom had mutually agreed to keep their finances separate when they married. So this was not even an issue. But here was Mom behaving like a spy on a secret mission. She'd place her fingers on her lips and whisper "Shh—Don't say a word to Beryl about this."

On one hand Mom was defiantly sneaking behind Beryl's back, but on the other hand he was the one she seemed to trust the most to take care of her. Her growing dependence on Beryl was becoming more obvious by the day. Beryl kept careful track of all the medications she was taking; making sure she received the proper dosage of the morning, noon, and night meds. He faithfully did this, despite the fact that Mom frequently fought against taking them. She would ask "What do I need those for?" Or "No, I'm not taking that," shaking her head vehemently. Beryl persisted in encouraging her. Eventually she would swallow her pills, then smile sweetly at him saying "Thank you, Beryl."

Beryl also helped Mom pick out what to wear every day, as this decision-making task was becoming more difficult. At this point she still dressed herself, but sometimes she came out of the bedroom with her shirt on backwards or her pants inside out. Beryl would patiently take her back in and help her redress. He also reminded her to brush her teeth and comb her hair. Sometimes she would forget what to do, and Beryl would show her how to put the paste on the toothbrush to get her started. Once when I was visiting I recall Mom emerging from the bathroom with streaks of toothpaste in her hair. She had mistakenly squeezed toothpaste all over Beryl's hairbrush and used it to brush hers! Together, Beryl and I quietly cleaned up the mess and redirected her. Rarely, did I ever hear him express exasperation towards her increasingly difficult behavior.

Once breakfast was over (Beryl also was preparing all the meals by now) and they were both dressed and ready for the day, the rest of the morning loomed before them. Beryl had so many interests which I will elaborate on later. Suffice it to say here, that he was content staying home engaged in his many hobbies. Mom, however, had lost the ability to continue on with *her* interests. She simply did not have the attention span or the memory of how to do things that had previously kept her occupied. This made her restless and demanding. "I'm tired of sitting here all day," she'd complain. "Let's go shopping at Thrifty Acres."

Beryl would try to delay the outing. "We'll go a little later. Right now I'm busy. Why don't you work on your word search puzzle?"

This would pacify her for only a short time. A few minutes later Mom would again demand "Let's go shopping!"

This would go on until Beryl finally gave in. Then, they would get into his car and head out to the store. Once inside, after walking around for only a few minutes, Mom would declare loudly "Let's go home!" The phrase "patience of a saint" comes to mind when I think of Beryl's tolerance.

Lori and Emily began taking Mom on shopping outings every Saturday morning to try to help out in this regard. Lori related to me how frustrated she would feel during the car ride to the store. Mom would ask "Where are we going?" Lori responded by telling her the name of the store. In only a matter of a few seconds Mom would repeat the question "Where are we going?" And Lori would give the same response. This continued on until they reached their destination.

"I know Mom couldn't remember that she kept asking me the same question over and over," she told me. "I *know* she couldn't help it, but by the umpteenth time of responding I was ready to lose it!" Emily, sensing her mom's frustration, would gently pat her arm to keep her calm. At the same time, she tried to engage her Grandma Helen in conversation to divert her attention. Emily was very perceptive at just what needed to be said in the right tone and was always able to diffuse a frustrating situation for Lori. These Saturday shopping outings gave Beryl of few more hours of much needed time to himself.

During the week, when she wasn't at the adult day care and the two of them were home alone together, Mom would follow Beryl around constantly. It was almost as if she was afraid to be alone in a room by herself. Beryl, on the contrary, needed to get away from the constant togetherness. He would direct her to a T.V. show or encourage her to take a nap and then try to escape for some quiet time spent working in his workshop. Invariably, after only a few minutes of solitude, Mom would show up and ask "What cha doin?" It was at this time that her days spent in adult day care were increased with no resistance from Beryl.

Lori and I were both trying to do whatever we could to lend a hand. Living so close, Lori and Paul would stop over frequently to help out in whatever way was needed. Often they would walk up the street with their two dogs in tow. Laughing at the dogs' antics provided needed relief for everyone. (Fergie, a wire-haired terrier, was Mom's favorite.) Ray and I were making more trips to Michigan as well, and sometimes I would come for more extended visits by myself. While I was there I would try to do as much cooking (preparing left-overs to be frozen and used later) and cleaning as possible. It was apparent that not much cleaning was being done. It was very difficult for Beryl with his limited mobility and Mom had abandoned any attempts at dusting the living room or cleaning the bathroom. It was time to seek out more help.

Our family all agreed that some kind of a home health care service would be very beneficial. We were looking for someone to come into their home a few days a week to do some light housekeeping, laundry, perhaps a little cooking. We also thought if we could coordinate the schedule, so that Mom would also be home at least one of those days, then the aid could give her a bath. Keeping my mother clean was becoming a MAJOR ISSUE.

For whatever reason, Mom resisted taking a bath. She had always kept herself looking nice and well groomed. So why the big fuss over getting into a bathtub now? Was she afraid of the water? Sometimes it almost seemed so. Or did she just not like the feeling of water running over her? I've talked with other caregivers who have had similar experiences and our mom's reaction seems quite typical. But knowing this didn't help solve the problem. Lori had been coming over as much as possible to help Mom bathe, as I did whenever I visited or when Mom came to my home. Memories of "The Battles of the Bath" are not pleasant ones for me (and I'm sure are not pleasant ones for my sister either). I can remember one time in particular when Mom was being extremely stubborn. As I attempted to get her into the tub, she put up a wall of feisty resistance.

"Why do I need to do that?" she complained.
"Because you haven't bathed in several days and you need to get clean," I explained. "Your skin is becoming greasy and you need to wash up so you smell fresh."
"No!" She shook her head firmly.
"Come on, Mom, I'll help you," I said as I took her arm and tried to guide her toward the tub.

"I said NO!" She planted her feet, gave me a look of angry determination, and swatted my arm.

Then I lost my temper. "Look, we can stay in the bathroom all day if you like. But we are *not* leaving here until you have had a bath! It's up to you." I felt like I was dealing with an unreasonable, defiant child, instead of my mother!

We both stood glaring at each other at an impasse for a few minutes. Then Mom relented and let me help her into the tub. I tried to relax her by talking her through the bath. By telling her exactly what I was going to do next, and getting it done as quickly as possible. Finally, she was clean and ready to go until it was time for the next battle.

This was only one example of many that led our family to seek some much needed home health care assistance. Beryl looked into what was available and made all the arrangements. We all sighed in relief. Another problem solved, we thought. Until the first day the worker showed up to find Mom standing firmly at the door with her arms crossed, barring her entrance!

Eventually Mom was persuaded that it was o.k. to allow this stranger into her home. This service proved to be very helpful, especially for Beryl, in relieving some of his load. It didn't always run smoothly, though. Some days Mom was more agreeable than others.

And to complicate matters, sometimes employees were replaced. Mom would just start getting used to an individual and then someone new would show up. Then it was back to square one—more resistance and uncooperative behavior. This whole notion of Mom actively sabotaging our attempts to find solutions was extremely frustrating!

The arrangement with home health care had its ups and downs, but nevertheless continued on for many months. That is, until the day yet another new person appeared and made the mistake of trying to give Mom a bath the first day they met. Mom's resistance came in the form of a kick in the shins. Beryl was informed later that day that the home health agency's association with our family was over. We were on our own again.

******

It was around this time that I began taking Mom home with me for week-long visits. When I first approached Beryl about this, I wasn't sure how he would react, but he readily accepted my offer. We both agreed that it would be good for Mom to have a change of scenery, as well as providing a needed break for Beryl. So from time to time I would take off from work and Mom would be sent along with us to Wisconsin.

Other than the bath time battles that I mentioned, I have some very warm memories of our time spent together. I always tried to plan ahead for some special activities that we could share during these visits. Sometimes Mom would express a child-like wonder at something that she had obviously done before, but her memory deficit made it seem like she was doing it for the very first time.

A walk through the woods at Kohler Terre Andre State Park brought exclamations of awe as she gazed at the tall trees and foliage around her. She kept repeating over and over again "I've *never* seen anything like this!"

Helping to bake Christmas cookies and decorate the tree brought smiles and laughter. "Isn't it beautiful?" she asked, when the tree was finally adorned in all its finery.

Visiting a local restaurant for coffee and a piece of coconut cream pie brought sighs of contentment. Mom *loved* coconut. (She once told me that, as a child, whenever she was given a little spending money for candy, Mom would always purchase a small bag of coconut instead). Anyway, Mom would savor each bite of the pie and say "Mmm—this is so good." as if she had never tasted anything quite like it.

Sometimes we took outings. On one of her first visits, we took a bus trip to a Dinner/Theatre establishment a few hours away to see "Joseph and the Amazing Technicolor Dream Coat". Mom had always loved musicals and I thought she would really enjoy this play. This turned out to be a mistake. Although "Joseph" is actually a short play, compared to most, for my mom it was still too long. She just did not have the attention span to sit for any extended period of time. Also, it was too complex of a concept for her to grasp. Those familiar with this play know that different styles of music and matching costuming are used to tell the Biblical story of Joseph in the Old Testament. Mom kept whispering comments like "Why are they wearing cowboy hats and boots? No one dressed like that in Joseph's Day!" and "What is Elvis doing there? What does he have to do with Joseph?" It was just too confusing and made no sense to her. I tried to whisper an explanation to no avail.

A friend of mine told me of a similar experience she had when she tried to take her mother (also in early stages of Alzheimer's) to "The Sound of Music". Although this had always been her mom's favorite play, by the second act she was sighing loudly all the way to the end.

After that experience at the play, Mom and I stuck to shorter outings that remained close to home. Like the time I took her (again at Christmas-time) to the Sheboygan Historical Museum to view the animated figures of animals and Santa's helpers that had once been in the display window of the old

Prange's Department Store. This had been the delight of children of all ages in bygone years. I can remember taking my own kids to see the display after it had been moved to Prange's basement. Mike, Angie, and Dan always loved talking to "Bruce the Spruce" and watching the animated figures. When I told Mom that we would be visiting this Christmas display that had been moved to the museum, she wrinkled her brow and asked "What's Christmas?"

After I recovered from the initial shock of hearing that question, I tried to briefly explain. My mother has always been a very spiritual woman and the thought that she did not remember a Christian event as momentous as Christmas was shocking to me. After all, she was the one who taught *me* the real meaning of Christmas, and now this, too, was a lost memory to her. Anyway, eventually we did go to the museum. And Mom's reaction was of pure delight, laughing and pointing at the moving figures and exclaiming, "Would you look at that?"

When we didn't have something special planned, I found it to be helpful to stick to a daily schedule. People with Alzheimer's tend to find comfort in familiar routines. We started our day with breakfast and, of course, coffee. (Mom has always been a big coffee drinker). Then we would head out for a short outing—shopping, taking a walk, or attending my dance class. Mom would sit in the back of the gym while I exercised. She kept herself busy with one of her word search puzzles. By the end of the session she had lost interest, but she always showed me all of the words she had found and seemed very proud of her accomplishment.

Next we headed home just in time for "The Price is Right" (her favorite game show) and more coffee. After lunch we would each claim a separate couch for a little nap. Once Mom fell asleep I would try to quietly get up to do some laundry or cleaning. It was amazing how she would seem to sense when I left the room and would immediately come looking for me, as she did with Beryl at home. In the mid afternoon, we would usually go out for a short ride, before returning home to fix supper.

By night-time you'd think Mom would be ready for bed. I know I was tired! On one occasion, I made the mistake of getting her into bed too early. I heard some rustlings coming from her room in the middle of the night. When I went to check, she was sitting primly on the edge of the bed totally dressed and ready to begin the day!
"Mom, what are you doing?" I asked. "It's too early to be up."
"Why?"
"Well, because it's 2 a.m. You should be back in bed."
"Why?"
"It's still dark outside. Everyone else is sleeping too. We won't be up for several more hours."

I eventually convinced her to rest longer (albeit fully clothed) by lying down with her until she fell asleep again. After that I was careful not to send her to bed too early!

During Mom's visits, I spent most of the time with her exclusively. It was very hard to get any work done around the house or have any time to myself. If I would pick up a book to read she would ask "Why do you want to look at that?" If I would try to dust or vacuum she would come looking for me saying "That looks clean enough!"

By the end of the week I was tired and ready to give Mom back to Beryl. I found it so sweet that he was just as ready to *take* her. We would usually meet up at a McDonalds just over the Michigan border. It was obvious by the way they embraced, that they were both happy to be together again. But I couldn't help but ask myself "How does Beryl do it, day after day?" I knew the time was coming when we would all have to prepare for another major change.

Helen with Her First Family

Ralph and Howa-Deenie

Helen's 70th Birthday Party – Lil (Itily May) in back

Back Row: Brothers Harold, John, Melvin, Ralph
Front Row: Lily, Grandma Effie Boyer, Helen

Helen with Her Girls

Brenda

Lori

Christmas in Sheboygan

WHO'S DANNY WRESTLE?

This might be a good place to take a break and laugh a little. There are so many sad and frustrating times that a family and their loved ones endure at the hands of Alzheimer's, that it's worthwhile to sit back, take a deep breath, and actually laugh at some of the humorous experiences that happen along the way.

The first story I'll share involves one of our family's favorite activities—eating. Mom had taught Lori and me how to make good, nutritious home-cooked meals and we both have cooked plenty of them in our lives! But it's nice on occasion to go out-to-eat. Lori's family usually goes out for a bite on Friday nights, while Ray and I have designated Saturday as our "no cooking" night. It was on one such evening when Mom, Beryl, Lori's family, and I all decided to go out for a bite at one of their favorite Portage restaurants.

Going to restaurants with Mom became increasingly difficult as time went on. But our family tried to get her out into the community as much as possible. At first we noticed she seemed to have trouble deciding what to order. Perhaps looking at the extensive menu was just to overwhelming for her. So, one of us would read part of it and explain the entrees. In the early part of this disease, Mom was able to make her own selection as long as she wasn't given too many choices. As time went on and decisions became more difficult, we limited her choice to two entrees that we knew she liked. "Would you like country fried steak with mashed potatoes or fried shrimp with a baked potato?" Eventually even this became too confusing and we had to order a meal for her with no choice provided. Anyway, at this point Mom was still fairly independent. She was capable of making menu choices and seemed to enjoy spending a night out with the family. She could carry on basic conversations and still liked to joke around.

When we arrived at the restaurant, it was very busy. Although we had reservations, we still had to wait a while before being seated. The hostess informed us that some patrons were just finishing their meal and their table would be ready for us shortly. After waiting for only a few minutes, two VERY LARGE men emerged from the dining room. They both had huge bellies that drooped far over their belts. They saw us waiting and in a friendly manner bellowed out "Don't worry—we saved you some food!"

Mom, in her attempt to be congenial back, responded even louder "WELL IT SURE DOESN'T LOOK LIKE IT!"

While the rest of us looked down wishing for a hole in the floor to temporarily swallow us, Mom sat there grinning at her "joke".

******

Another humorous incident demonstrates how the meaning of words can be so easily misconstrued.

Ray and I were taking Mom home for a visit to Wisconsin. I had scooted into the back seat with Mom to keep her company and see that she didn't unfasten her seat belt. I was chatting away, telling her about all the activities I had planned for the upcoming week. She seemed to be half-listening, not showing much interest in my prattle. My son, Dan, was going to participate in one of his high school wrestling meets during that week and we had planned on attending. After going through a long litany of upcoming activities, I ended with "And then on Thursday night, we're going to see Danny wrestle."

Now I had Mom's attention. She turned to me, wrinkled her nose, and with a look of total befuddlement on her face asked "Who's Danny Wrestle?"

I caught Ray's laughing eyes looking at me in the rear view mirror, as if to say "O.K., handle that one." To which I did as best as I could. After hearing my explanation that I was talking about her grandson, Danny Springhetti, and that we were going to *watch* him in a wrestling meet, Mom just looked at me with disgust and turned her head facing forward again. I decided then that riding along in a comfortable silence was preferable to mindless chatter. We had a quiet ride the rest of the way home.

******

Another incident I recall happened on yet another one of Mom's visits. Ray and I had driven all the way to Michigan to pick her up, and we were going to return on the same day. That meant a ten hour drive for us, round trip, so we didn't have a lot of time to stick around to visit with Beryl. When we arrived, Beryl was waiting with her suitcase packed and ready to go.

He assured us that he had packed plenty of clothing, but was sorry that he couldn't find her favorite pair of fuchsia-colored slacks. The top that she was wearing that day was a match to them. It had fuchsia and purple trim. Beryl knew that Mom used to be fussy about matching outfits, but the purple slacks she was wearing also went with her top. So they would have to do.

"I just don't know what she did with those bright pink slacks. We looked all over for them. I kept asking Helen where she put them, but who knows?" He just shrugged. I could understand his dilemma. Mom was taking things out of drawers and misplacing them in all kinds of odd places those days.

"Don't worry about it, Beryl," I assured him. "I'm sure she has plenty of slacks packed and we can even go shopping this week to see if we can replace those pink ones."

So along we went. It was a long drive, but we stopped for dinner along the way. By the time we finally arrived in Wisconsin it was fairly late and I told Mom it was time to get ready for bed.
"Why?" Mom asked, as I tried to help her.
"It's late and time to get your pajamas on to go to bed".
"No, I'll just keep these on," she insisted pointing to what she was wearing.
"You can't sleep in your clothes!"
"Why not?"
"Because they will get all wrinkled in bed; and besides, you'll be more comfortable in your pajamas."
"No," she insisted with that very familiar shake of her head.
I was tired and in no mood for this bedtime battle. "Why did our visit have to start out like this?" I thought.
"Mom, let me help you," I said, reaching for her pants.
"NO!" she exclaimed, holding tight to the elastic waistband.

But I grabbed harder and pulled them down quickly in exasperation. What I saw next, had me collapsing on the bed in uncontrollable laughter. For there, underneath her purple slacks, were the favorite fuchsia ones that Beryl had searched so hard for! I had this mental picture of Beryl searching high and low, with Mom traipsing alongside him, while he repeatedly asked her where she had put her slacks. All along they were within arm's reach. She was wearing them!

Mom sat down next to me on the bed and started laughing too. I'm sure she didn't know what was so funny. But laughter is contagious and Mom loved to laugh, so it was understandable that she would join in. We both had a good laugh together and then proceeded to get ready for bed. It was a good start to her visit after all.

******

Lori related this next incident to me. My sister works in a school library, so she always has her summers off. During this particular summer, Mom had been going through that phase where she was bored and restless at home. On the days when she didn't attend day care, Mom took the opportunity to walk down the street to visit Lori—several times a day! This particular day was a record setter. Lori had counted ten times when Mom showed up at her door. She never stayed long. Just long enough to say "hi" and pet the dogs, then she would head off back up the street to return home to see Beryl. Back and forth she went all day long.

At the end of this day, Lori was tired and ready to put her feet up. She finished her supper dishes and carried the garbage out. Then, she stopped in amazement trying to figure out what she was seeing. Her recycle bin was *loaded to the brim* with sticks and parts of tree branches! "Where in the world did these come from?" she thought. She found out the next day as she watched Mom approach the house. Along came Mom; her arms loaded with sticks, leaves, and branches that had apparently been collected on her stroll down the street. A matching bin of refuse was later found at her house where she had apparently deposited similar loads on her trips back *up* the street. Mom was not one to fuss with cleaning the house, mind you. But she was developing a compulsion to keep the great outdoors tidy!

******

Before the onset of Alzheimer's, Mom had always preferred outdoor chores (mowing the lawn, trimming hedges, raking leaves etc.) to house cleaning inside. So it was not too surprising that now she loved spending time outside ridding the environment of any foreign objects that she found objectionable. She was frequently seen throwing sticks over her backyard fence into the field behind her house. This was a harmless enough hobby, as long as she stayed on her own property. However, problems arose when this activity extended into others' yards. This leads to another story.

Mom's next door neighbors were trying to grow grass on a bald patch of their lawn. They had planted grass seed and then spread straw over the area to protect it. This did not pass Mom's inspection, and she took it upon herself to rid the neighbors' lawn of that pesky straw. One can imagine Beryl's dismay when he looked out the window and saw Mom trampling all over the newly planted grass and busily picking up its protective covering. He hurried out (as quickly as Beryl could "hurry") and quickly ushered Mom back into their house. "You can't do that, Helen!" he exclaimed. To which Mom provided her standard response "Why?" Beryl had to keep a very close eye on her after that, because every time he turned around he would catch her heading back out to clean up the mess. Although the Clarks never said a word, I'm sure they noticed the increased activity in their yard. By the time that bald patch had finally grown grass, there was more than one interested party breathing a sigh of relief.

These are just a few examples of the many humorous moments we have encountered along this long road.

Beryl and Helen in Her Fuchsia Slacks

Helen Enjoyed Being Outside

ASSISTED LIVING

The Decision and Search

It was becoming more and more apparent that Mom's situation at home was deteriorating. We had exhausted all means of outside assistance that enabled Mom to remain in her own home for as long as she did. In fact, we began receiving tactful hints from the day care that perhaps it was time to think about placing her in a long term care facility that was more equipped to deal with Mom's declining condition. Although we knew this was true, the next step was a gut wrenching one to take, especially for Beryl.

Lori and I were amazed that Beryl was able to shoulder the burden of Mom's care for so long. We remained sensitive about his feelings, not wanting to "take over" and make a decision he wasn't ready for. After all, we remembered his initial reaction when he discovered we had power of attorney over Mom. I can't count the number of times we said something like this: "Beryl, you have to tell us when this becomes too much for you to handle. Do you want us to begin searching for other arrangements?"

Although Beryl seemed to get some relief at unburdening his frustrations, when it came to finding a solution, he backed off. "No, it does get tiring at times, but so far we're still managing."

This went on for some time—perhaps too long. It finally occurred to me that Beryl was really waiting for Lori and me to make that decision for him. It was just too painful for him to take the next step. On one of my visits I could clearly see that the home situation was becoming impossible for Beryl to handle. So, Lori and I took the bull by the horns so to speak. When we found a few moments without Mom present we simply stated, "Beryl, it's time." He looked down and sadly nodded his head in agreement. So our search began.

The united team of Beryl, Lori, and Brenda kicked into high gear again to find a new home for Mom. I say "home" because that is exactly how we looked at it. None of us wanted to feel like we were shoving Mom off into some cold, institutionalized care facility. We were looking for a place that most resembled a home setting, yet could provide her with the daily care that was becoming impossible for us. This led us to touring various assisted living centers.

The place we eventually chose was located in a separate building from the main assisted living center. This smaller building only housed about 30 residents and catered exclusively to "memory" disorders. All the residents there had Alzheimer's or other related dementias. The staff had plenty of experience helping people like Mom. From what we were able to observe, they seemed to treat the residents with compassion and dignity. This was the most important factor to us.

The director showed us around and we were impressed with what we saw. Basically, the building was clean and had the "homey" atmosphere that we wanted. It was constructed around an outdoor courtyard in the center, that the residents had free access to in good weather. We knew Mom would love keeping that courtyard clean! There were two small dining areas (plus a separate one for if family wanted to visit in private during meal time), a cheerful sun room, TV lounge, even a dress-up area furnished with hats and accessories for residents' use. Mom would have her own bedroom and bath and there was plenty of room for her to wander freely without getting lost. The facility was state licensed and had a good security system. We were also shown the monthly calendar of events with daily activities to promote a stimulating environment. Perhaps the final clincher was that it was located around two miles from Beryl and Lori! We all agreed that this was where we wanted Mom placed. It was to be her home for the next five years.

Moving In

Preparations were made for the big move. Besides signing all the necessary papers and getting the proper medical clearance, we had to prepare Mom. This was not as hard as it may seem. By this time, Mom didn't always seem to understand what was said to her. She would often seem to drift off in her mind, staring blankly ahead. Sometimes one could bring her attention back, and sometimes not. Her responses to conversations were definitely diminishing as well. So I didn't really expect that we would get much of a reaction when we explained the situation. I was right about that.

On the day before the move, I sat Mom down next to me on the couch and explained as simply as I could that she would soon be living in a new place. I assured her that she would still see Beryl (and Lori and me) since we would come to visit her in her new home. I explained that there would be nice people to help take care of her. That it would be similar to the day care center that she was used to, the main difference being that she would sleep there as well.

I seemed to have Mom's attention during the little talk. She nodded her head and said "O.K". I don't know how much she understood, but she most likely forgot everything I said within a few minutes of my explanation. Nevertheless, it was important to *me* that I at least made the attempt to prepare her. I knew that I could not in all good conscience take her to her new home, and just walk away. No way could I could leave her there without at least *trying* to explain it to her, whether she understood (and remembered) or not.

The next morning on July 9, 2005 Lori and I moved Mom into assisted living. Knowing it would be too difficult for Beryl, we had him say his good-by at their home. We had already moved most of her belongings the day before. Clothes to be worn in the summer months were neatly hung in her closet (with her name properly labeled on everything). Family pictures were strategically placed around the room. Lori had even brought in a favorite stuffed bear and familiar knick knacks to help Mom feel at home.

From this time on, Lori took on the first of many responsibilities as she oversaw Mom's care at assisted living. When summer turned into fall, she would pack up all of Mom's lighter clothing and bring other outfits that were appropriate to the cooler weather. She always made sure that Mom's room decorations were in tune with the season/holiday—constantly packing old ones away, replacing them with others to celebrate an upcoming event. Mom's room always looked updated and cheerful. She saw to it that Mom had warm sweaters, nightclothes, underwear and socks, and that all her toiletries remained well stocked. Although the Home did all the laundry, Lori checked Mom's room every time she visited to make sure she was not wanting for anything.

It was a slow, quiet time in the mid-afternoon when we arrived at the Home. Our first order of business was to show Mom her room. As we took her by the hand and led her toward it, Lori pointed out that Mom's room was located in the "pink" corridor. (Each hall was color coded a different color to help residents find their way). We opened the door to her room and pointed to where all her clothes were and showed her the pictures and personal items from home. Mom kept making comments like "Oh, that's very nice" and gave repeated affirmations as we asked "Do you like the bear set here on the bed?" Or "Is it o.k. to keep your nightgowns in this top drawer?" "Oh, yes," she said pleasantly, nodding her head. "That's just fine."

Next we took her on a tour of the building showing her all the different special areas and the courtyard. We explained how she would be able to wander around the Home without ever getting lost. Since the hallways dead-ended and the center part of the building was built around the courtyard in a circle, one could just keep walking around and around always ending up at the starting point. "How nice," she murmured.

Finally we all made our way back to the front lobby where we found several other residents gathered. They were all sitting in comfortable couches and chairs that were arranged in a semi-circle around a beautiful fireplace. A recreational assistant was playing a game of catch with a large beach ball. We joined the group and encouraged Mom to participate. Dora was calling each resident's name before throwing them the ball. When it became Mom's turn, Dora said,
"Do you want to play, Helen? Can you catch this?"
Mom caught the ball thrown her way. Then she promptly threw it back—hard.
"Wow! You're really good," Dora encouraged.
Mom smiled in response.

The game went on for awhile. Since mom seemed to be engaged in the activity, Lori and I made our move to leave. We caught the eye of an aid standing close by, so she could open the front door for us without tripping the alarm. We explained to Mom that she was to stay and finish the game. Then, after briefly kissing her on the cheek, telling her that we loved her, and reassuring her that we would be back soon, we left as quickly as possible.

Apparently, we weren't quick enough. As we left, I glanced back to see Mom following us. An aide was trying to escort her back into the building. Lori and I both knew that for us to turn back now would only prolong the pain. So, we raced to the car and began to drive away. Through our tears we saw a second aide come to the rescue of the first, as they both attempted to lead a struggling, kicking Helen back into the building. Lori drove to the nearest parking lot at a near-by grocery store. She put the car in park and we both bawled our eyes out.

What should we do now? We decided to return to the Home for our own piece of mind. When we arrived at the parking lot, all was quiet. We didn't see any staff out frantically looking for a runaway resident, so we assumed Mom had safely re-entered the building.

Once we returned home, Beryl and his son, Dave, were waiting. Dave had been stopping by to check on his dad from time to time. (Eventually he moved in with Beryl to help out as his health declined). Dave knew that this day would be devastating to Beryl, so he was there to lend support and planned to stay overnight. One look at our faces and they both knew we had gone through a tough time. I'll always be grateful for Dave's kind, supportive words. "You girls have been through a lot, but remember, you did the right thing."

After calling the Home to make sure Mom was, indeed, safe inside and had calmed down, Lori and I went down the street to her house. We ate some dinner. Afterwards we opened a bottle of wine and took two glasses with us into her hot tub in the back yard. We felt we deserved to relax. But in the back of our minds we were both wondering how Mom was doing on her first night in her new home.

The next morning presented me with a dilemma. I was to return to Wisconsin later that day, but I didn't want to leave without seeing Mom one more time. I still had the image of her being dragged back into the Home and I desperately wanted to replace it with a happier memory. Yet, on the other hand, I knew it could be a mistake. We had been advised by the director to keep our visits to a minimum for the first few weeks to give Mom a chance to adjust. I decided to take the chance.

I called ahead to let the staff know that I would be stopping by. When I arrived Mom was sitting by herself in the dining area reserved for family visits. She was eating her breakfast as I approached.
"Hi sweetie," I said giving her shoulder a squeeze. "How are you today?"
Mom looked up at me in surprise. "Oh, Hi!" she said. "I'm just fine. How are you?"
"I'm good too. Did you sleep well last night?"
"Yes I did," she affirmed as she continued eating.

We sat together as she finished her breakfast. I don't recall anything specific said after that. Just that we spent a comfortable, quiet time together. When it was time to leave, I kissed her and promised her that I would be back as soon as I could. She smiled and responded "O.K."
"Good by, Mom. I love you."
"I love you, too."

I was certainly pleasantly surprised by Mom's calm behavior. I had prepared myself for tears and her begging me to take her home. I had even rehearsed in my mind how I would handle it. Fortunately, there was none of that. Peace and acceptance seemed to be her demeanor. Could it be that Mom had already adjusted to her new home in only a matter of a day? I was flabbergasted, but at the same time immensely relieved.

I don't pretend to have the answer for why she accepted her new situation so readily. Perhaps for Mom her reality was only the here and now. Even the past of only one day ago was now a forgotten memory. This was where she belonged now. This was home to her. When I returned to my job, I asked my supervisor, Julie, what she made of it. Julie had years of experience in her job dealing with Alzheimer's issues and I respected her opinion. She just shook her head and said "You must have timed this move just right." Whatever the case, our family was blessed that Mom made such an easy transition to assisted living.

Life At The Home

The next five years seemed to fly by. We all settled into a new routine. Beryl and Lori visited Mom weekly. The burden of daily care was now off their shoulders. Although I'm sure Beryl missed Mom's presence, gradually he adjusted to their new separate living arrangement. He took advantage of every opportunity to visit and spend quality time with her. It wasn't the same as having her home, but he made the best of it.

Occasionally, Lori and Beryl would take Mom out for lunch, sometimes followed by a short visit home in the afternoon. When it was time to return her to the Home, Mom always went back willingly.

I had made a silent promise to myself to try to make it to Michigan once every other month to visit. I was usually accompanied by Ray or sometimes one of my kids. (Unlike my mother who had made that trip around Chicago when she was my age, I hesitated going alone, and still prefer company to this day). One by one they all eventually visited Grandma Helen in her new home. I was anxious to get their opinion, especially my daughter, Angie, who is an R.N. but had previously worked as a C.N.A. in a nursing home. She, along with the others, gave a resounding "thumbs up"; as did Paul, Emily, and Andy from Lori's family. It was reassuring to know that our families also felt that we had made the right decision.

Mom always appeared clean and well cared for. She settled into a nice routine herself. In the beginning she participated in activities and made some friends. There were two women in particular whom Mom gravitated to. Betty, Ann, and Mom spent hours walking the halls together, attempting to converse in their limited way. Their conversations often made no sense to the casual observer, but seemed to make perfect sense to them.

I recall one sweet incident with the three amigos. They were in the sunroom gathered around a bassinette, fussing over a doll. This event happened in the summer when Mom first arrived. The Home was air conditioned and sometimes it seemed a little cool, as is the case with air conditioning. The ladies all were wearing sweaters. But their concern was for the "baby". Betty looked at me and asked, "Do you suppose he's warm enough?" Mom and Anne echoed their concern, worry clearly etched on their faces. "I'm sure he's just fine," I reassured. Nevertheless, they tucked the blanket tighter around the doll's neck, before proceeding on their walk. Their mothering instinct was still preserved.

There aren't enough words to adequately describe the compassionate care provided by the staff. They did their best to provide a safe, nurturing atmosphere. All were well equipped to handle behavioral issues that inevitably arose when so many people with serious mental deficiencies lived together. Sometimes arguments would break out when a resident would wander into another's room and help themselves to something that didn't belong to them. Although clothing was labeled and every attempt was made to return possessions to their rightful owners, it was not uncommon to see Nancy shuffling along in Wanda's slippers, or for that matter, Mom wearing Bill's baseball cap. She was no stranger to visiting others' rooms uninvited either! It was truly one big, happy family, with share and share alike as the motto. Families learned quickly not to bring anything of any real value to the Home.

I like to buy Mom new clothes for her birthday or Mother's Day etc. At first I thought I should just buy inexpensive clothing at a discount store or even a second hand store. After all, food would be spilled on that new blouse, and who knows who would end up actually wearing it? I thought better of it. Mom had always taken pride in her appearance. She liked wearing matching sets of slacks and tops, bold colors being her preference. I thought why should that change now that she was dependent on someone else providing her wardrobe? Why shouldn't she get something nice and fresh and new? So I continued to shop at her favorite stores, buying the kinds of clothes I knew she liked. Of course, they were always carefully labeled, and I hoped for the best that *she* actually was the one to wear them. But if I happened to see someone else in her clothing, it was nothing to get upset about. Whatever happened was no big deal.

I have many pleasant memories of visits with Mom at assisted living. Sometimes Lori would come with me and the three of us would walk the halls together since this continued to be one of Mom's favorite activities. When she could no longer walk, we took her on wheelchair rides. Other times I would join her in various recreation activities. Mom and I especially enjoyed the musical "sing-alongs". During one of my early visits, an outside performer with a guitar led the group in song. By this time Mom was struggling with speech, but she could *sing* some memorized lyrics that somehow remained in her memory. Still other times, we would just sit quietly in the courtyard listening to nature's music of birds singing or breezes rustling tree leaves and wind chimes.

Our families tried to celebrate Mom's birthdays and holidays with her at the Home as much as possible. And it always made our visits special when we could get a few laughs from her. I recall one Christmas when my sister placed a reindeer headband on Mom and we all dressed up in similar antlers or silly hats. Immediately, her eyes crinkled up and her shoulders began shaking in laughter. I don't think she stopped smiling the whole time we were there!

There were many other humorous incidents that brought a chuckle from time to time. Like the time early-on when Mom and her co-conspirators tried to make a break and leave the facility. Of course the alarms went off and the three ladies were immediately detained.

Another time a resident, very much aware of the alarm system, tried to warn some visitors who were waiting for a staff person to let them in. He waved them back and shouted through the door. "Don't come in! Once you enter, they'll never let you out!"

Or how about when John came casually walking to the front lobby with nothing on but a shirt and his Depends? He kept asking everyone he met "Got a smoke?" One of the aides exclaimed, "John, where are your bottoms?" John stopped walking, looked over his shoulder, smacked his rear end, and said "Why…my bottom's right here!"

Yes, life at the Home was certainly interesting, for residents, staff, and visitors alike!

******

As mentioned previously, Lori has remained ever vigilant in seeing that Mom's needs are met. Her welfare has been a top priority from day one. This may be a good place to describe the relationship that Lori worked hard to develop with the staff at the assisted living home. I think the best way to describe it, is that Lori has always been Mom's *advocate* without being *adversarial*. That was so important in developing a relationship of trust and respect towards those who were responsible for Mom's daily care. Whenever Lori would observe something that bothered her, instead of jumping down someone's throat demanding "Why is this?" she would, instead, approach the subject diplomatically. Calmly bringing a concern to the attention of staff and seeking a resolution, before taking it to a higher authority, usually elicited the results Lori sought. Human nature proves that when people are treated with respect, they will respond in kind. My sister was wise to realize this.

One example was when Mom was inexplicably moved from her normal seat at the dining table. When Mom first arrived at the Home, she was still able to feed herself. She didn't always use a fork or spoon correctly, but managed to eat her meals independently. As time went on, however, this became increasingly difficult. Eventually, she reached the point where she needed assistance being fed and was moved to another dining room. Lori made it a habit to visit Mom whenever she could at a meal time so she could feed her. Family members of the other residents did the same. Lori became well acquainted with them and she described fellow diners and aids as being sort of like a mini support group in that dining room.

Mom shared a small table with one other lady who had become her newest "buddy". By this time neither Mom nor Molly could communicate verbally anymore. But they would acknowledge each other with their eyes, try to reach across the table to touch fingers, and sometimes talk back and forth in "jibberish" that only they understood. They were accustomed to and comfortable with each other. In fact, the entire feeding group in this room had become like family.

Anyway, one day when Lori arrived she discovered that Mom had been moved to another table in the first dining room and she was not happy about it! The reason isn't important and had nothing to do with Mom. Lori immediately got to the bottom of it, and let her strong feelings be known *in a nice way*. The next time Lori came to visit, Mom and Molly were together again at their table. Problem solved.

Through the years, as caregivers came and went, Lori made it a point to get to know them and develop a friendly relationship with each of them. She sought their advice and opinions as well as giving her own. I think the staff all came to see Lori as truly part of the team in Mom's care. In turn, they provided a tremendous amount of support to her. Years later, when Mom was moved into a nursing facility, saying good-by to the "family" at the assisted living center was more difficult for my sister than it was for Mom.

DNR Issues

One major decision our family had to make prior to Mom's admittance into assisted care was whether or not to sign a "Do Not Resuscitate" (DNR) order. Beryl, Lori and I were all in agreement that we did not want any extraordinary medical means applied to keep Mom alive. We knew from discussions with Mom, prior to her illness, that this would be her wish as well. Our understanding was that no machines would be utilized to keep Mom's heart beating or to keep her breathing. No CPR would ever be performed. We were signing permission to just let nature take its course in the progression of her disease. It seemed a cut and dried issue. Little did we know, then, how blurred the lines can become between what's considered "resuscitation" and what's considered "providing comfort".

A few months after Mom's arrival at the Home, Beryl received a phone call from the medical staff explaining that Mom had collapsed during one of her walks. It appeared that she had stopped breathing for a few seconds. Upon repositioning her onto her side, Mom began breathing again on her own. Since she had hit her head on the floor, the paramedics were called and they were preparing to transport her to the hospital to be checked out further. By the time her family met up with Mom in the emergency room, she was resting comfortably.

This was to be the first of many times when Beryl, Lori, and Paul would spend hours in the ER with Mom after one of her "spells". Only to be told much later that nothing specific was found to have caused her to faint and that she could return to the Home. The possibility that she had suffered a mini stroke, heart attack, or seizure had all been eventually ruled out after undergoing medical tests. Yet, Mom continued to experience these blackouts from time to time. It was believed that occasionally her oxygen level took a dive (for whatever unknown reason) causing her to pass out.

On one particular occasion, years later, Mom's breathing seemed to stop for a longer amount of time than usual during another one of these episodes. She had actually begun to turn blue. By this time Lori had become the main contact person (after Beryl's death) and she was immediately called. Anyway, the medical staff informed Lori that they had been afraid that they were "going to lose" Mom during this episode. They explained that, if the paramedics hadn't arrived just when they did to give her some oxygen, it may have been too late.

The question Lori and I both wondered was "Why, then, was Mom resuscitated when we had specifically signed the DNR papers?" It was explained to us that providing oxygen was not the same as CPR. Mom had apparently still been breathing, if very slightly. Giving oxygen was providing comfort care, not resuscitating her. Of course we wanted our mother made comfortable. But this forced us to deal head on with our own conflicting feelings about Mom's life and death.

All kinds of questions swirled around our heads. If there had been no intervention, would Mom have passed on to a better life? Or would she have survived the episode with further brain damage making her worse off in *this* life than she is now? And how can Lori and I even be thinking of our mother's demise? What kind of daughters are we, anyway, almost wishing she had passed on? Yet in our hearts, through our faith, we knew that a better life awaited her. A life so much better than this twilight existence she was trapped in. We were told that should we decide to deny the oxygen support in the future, more papers would have to be signed again. Lori and I both were haunted by the feeling that we were being asked to sign a permission slip approving our mother's imminent death over and over again. Our emotions were in turmoil and we were so conflicted about the right course of action.

These issues are difficult and have been faced by countless families like ours who have found themselves in similar situations. There are no easy answers. Thankfully, Lori and I had each other to talk things through. We also had support from our families. Also, at this point, Hospice came into our lives and proved to be such a blessing.

I remember visiting Mom around this time, just before Hospice began providing that support. As I approached her in her wheelchair, I almost didn't recognize my own mother! She was slumped over, drooling, and totally unresponsive as I kept patting her cheek and calling out to her. She eventually opened her eyes a little, but showed no recognition of me at all. I didn't stay long. When I returned to my sister's house, I broke down. "She looked so bad, today. I can't stand seeing Mom like this!" I cried.

It was shortly after this that Hospice stepped in, and along with a doctor that they recommended, adjusted her medication. We didn't realize it, but Mom was being over medicated. All it took was getting her off some of the pills she had been taking, to get her more alert. The next time I visited, her bright blue eyes gazed back at me. She was wide awake and much more responsive. Ray and I were even able to get a few giggles out of her. What a difference!

Besides checking up on Mom, the hospice worker was a tremendous support to Lori. She told me how Susan would often call, just to ask how Lori was doing and if there was anything she could do to help. Just having a professional willing to talk as long as Lori needed to vent fears and frustrations was such a help to my sister.

Talking with professionals and with each other helped Lori and me sort out our feelings and make yet more decisions. Since then we have also had to specifically state whether or not we wish to have a feeding tube inserted when the time comes that Mom stops eating. As I said previously, there are no easy answers when it comes to life or death and "comfort issues". But I definitely feel those decisions should be made by the family. I would certainly trust most families to act in the best interest of a loved one over some hospital/government bureaucrat who may be more interested the cost effectiveness of treatment. The elderly, sick, and handicapped deserve better than that. Whatever decisions are made, I feel strongly that *life* is God's great gift to us and that *life* (from birth to death) should be respected above all else.

So Lori and I are at peace with our decisions. Mom continues to have black outs occasionally. But staff responds according to our requests, and is usually able to keep her at her own facility, without a needless trip to the hospital. She seems comfortable and is well cared for. For now, we all persevere.

Helen and Lori Having Silly Fun

Lori and Brenda Visiting Helen Shortly After One of her "Spells"

BERYL

At this point I'd like to say a little more about Mom's second husband, Beryl. The two met at a Widow/Widowers support group after they had each lost their spouse. When Mom first introduced Beryl to our family, I think she was a little nervous about our reaction. She wasn't sure what we would think of her developing a relationship with another man other than our dad. After all, Mom and Dad had been married for over 40 years, and no one could ever replace Dad in our hearts. As mentioned previously, Lori and I never thought of Beryl as a father figure, but we eventually did come to love him for who he was in his own right. We were happy that Mom had found love and companionship again.

Beryl was eleven years older than our mom. But you would never know it. He had a youthful exuberance and quick wit that belied his age. His interests were many. Early on in their marriage, Beryl convinced Mom to take organ lessons with him (and for a short while she was able to share that interest). Beryl owned his own organ and had become quite accomplished at playing. His organ even had a recording feature so he could listen to his created music over and over again.

Woodworking was another one of Beryl's talents. He loved making things to give away to others. Decorative shelves, coat racks, small cabinets, benches were just a few of his creations. If one of his kids or grandchildren mentioned something they needed, the words were barely out of their mouths, before Beryl was already making plans for its construction. Our own home is adorned with some of his gifts to us. He took well deserved pride in his high craftsmanship.

Beryl was a patient, kind man who never seemed to get rattled by life's surprises. His dry sense of humor seemed to get him through a lot of frustrating situations. One example that comes to mind is when Mom accidently drove his car through her garage door. This occurred shortly before their marriage. Mom was driving Beryl back to her home in his car after he underwent a minor medical procedure. After she drove up the steep incline of her driveway, Mom realized she didn't have the remote control to open the garage door. She knew she would have to open it by pressing the button inside the garage. It's not clear why, but somehow her foot had slipped off of the brake. Anyway, in preparation to exit the car, she planned to step on the brake and put the car in park. But instead of stomping the brake, she floored the gas pedal! The car lurched forward, crashing through the garage door. It all happened so quickly that Mom was in shock. She kept saying over and over, "What happened? What happened?"

To which Beryl responded in his normal unflappable manner. "Well," he calmly drawled, "you just drove *my* car through *your* garage door." Yup, that's what happened all right. It was so typical of Beryl to just dryly state the facts with tongue in cheek.

As time went on, Beryl's "minor medical procedures" became more major problems. It's not necessary to go into all that he endured, but he had plenty of physical challenges. Despite his troubles, he rarely complained. Instead, Beryl found ways to overcome difficulties and adapt to situations. Limited mobility really became an issue in the last year of his life. It reached the point where it was too hard for him to visit Mom anymore. Except for doctor's appointments, he basically became home bound. This limitation required even more cheerful adaptation on his part. Beryl had a comfortable office chair set up at the kitchen table. Surrounding him, within arm's reach, were his remote control (for a kitchen T.V. that faced him), a portable phone, radio, stacks of mail carefully sorted, a letter opener, magazines, word puzzles, a magnifying glass, and a few snacks. After he died, our family could not enter the house without visualizing Beryl sitting there in control at what we fondly dubbed his "command post".

Beryl died on March 11, 2008. His children were at his side and he also asked to see Lori and Paul. Lori called me a few hours after their visit to tearfully say "His daughter just called to tell us he's gone."

By this time, Mom was no longer leaving the Home for outside outings. She and Beryl had not been able to visit with one another for some time now. Although Lori knew that Mom would not remember or understand, Lori had to at least try to explain to her that her husband had passed away. Lori's family and mine all attended the funeral service. After introducing myself and my sister (who was at my side) I delivered the following eulogy:

We would like to say a few words about Beryl on behalf of our mom who can't be here today.

Our family has known Beryl for over ten years now. From the first time we met him, we knew we couldn't have picked a better husband for Mom. She had been lonely since our dad died in 1991. Then she met Beryl at a Widow/Widowers' group and they hit it off from the start. We were all happy for them when they eventually married on Aug. 22, 1998. Beryl filled Mom's life with happiness, love, and laughter again. Lori and I both regret that they didn't have more time together when they both enjoyed good health. Beryl and Mom were so compatible. I think they both looked forward to traveling and enjoying each other's company in their golden years.

But, as fate would have it, Mom developed Alzheimer's early into their marriage and Beryl became more than her husband—he became her main caregiver. It certainly wasn't something he signed on for, but he accepted the commitment willingly and lovingly. He was so patient and took such good care of her. Our family will always be grateful to him for that. Even when she became more difficult (and she would come to visit me for a week at a time) I could tell Beryl missed her and was ready for her to come home. It broke his heart when he had to finally let her go into assisted living.

Over the years that I have known him, Beryl has always been a kind, soft spoken man with a twinkle in his eye, especially when he was telling one of his jokes. He liked to make them up using a play on words. And nobody laughed harder at his jokes than he did himself!

I talked to him recently when he was in the hospital and he repeated a typical "Beryl" joke that he had been telling his nurses. We both laughed and I said "Beryl, I can see you haven't lost your sense of humor." To which he replied "When I lose my sense of humor, that will be the end of me." Well, he kept that sense of humor to the end. Maybe that's why he remained so cheerful, despite all of the physical problems he endured these past few years.

I know I speak for Mom and all our family when I say that Beryl was a wonderful man, and a blessing to all who knew and loved him. We will all miss him very much.

Family Group at Beryl and Helen's Wedding

SISTERS

Lori

How do I begin to attempt to cover everything that my sister has done for my Mom over the past several years? Even when Beryl was alive, Lori was the main "caretaker" of Mom's every need. I have already described how she has stayed on top of situations at assisted living, (and now at the nursing home) to be Mom's advocate. Mom can no longer speak for herself, but Lori can speak for her. And believe me she does!

Soon after Mom was transferred to the facility where she lives now, my sister was put to the test of proving that she truly was a champion of Mom's rights. When Mom was still at assisted living, some of her funds went towards purchasing a hospital bed and a new wheelchair. The bed had controls, tilting it up or down to make it easier to transfer her in and out of bed, as well as side rails to prevent her from falling out. Since the nursing home came equipped with its own hospital bed, Lori donated Mom's to the assisted living home. However, she made sure that the wheelchair went along with Mom. This wheelchair, I suppose, wasn't anything special by wheelchair standards. But it was *hers*—the one she was accustomed to. It was well padded and fit her frame perfectly. Mom always seemed very comfortable resting in it. Lori had even personalized it by placing decorative stickers on it.

During one of Lori's visits after the move, she noticed right away that Mom had been placed in an old ill-fitting wheelchair. She asked around trying to find out what had happened to Mom's chair, with promises from staff that they would try to find where it was. "Was someone else using Mom's chair by mistake?" Lori wondered. The next time she arrived to find Mom slumped over in that same rickety-wheeled wagon, she made her displeasure known, *this time perhaps in not such a nice way*! The staff was just as perplexed, but eventually did get to the bottom of it.

Lori called me to angrily report that the medical supply company that Mom's chair had been purchased from, had reclaimed it. According to their records, it was loaned to her due to her association with Hospice at the time she was at assisted living. (Lori insisted that the money was withdrawn from Mom's account to pay for it the same time the hospital bed was purchased). Anyway, upon Mom's transfer, a representative showed up at her nursing home and reclaimed it without saying a word to Lori.

"Mom has been using that chair for years!" Lori exclaimed. "I *know* we paid for it. How can they do that to her? Our mother has had so many losses with this Alzheimer's, and now this is taken this away too? Her chair was one of the few comforts she has left and now someone just comes along and practically rips it out from under her!! Well, we'll just see about that!"

My sister's words and tone sounded strangely familiar. In reminded me of the time Mom ripped that dress off the mannequin in my behalf. Lori was proving to have some of Mom's feistiness when it came to defending a loved one's best interests. Several phone calls later, Lori was triumphant! The chair was back where it belonged! Mom could keep it for the rest of her life. No further charges were incurred. Way to go Lori! Just as Mom was once nicknamed "Slugger" for a past action of defense, perhaps from now on, Lori should be known as the "Wheelchair Warrior"!

This is just one example of many when Lori has intervened in Mom's behalf. She has also handled Mom's bills, occasionally questioning why a charge was made for this or that. My sister's stress level has been high at times, understandably so. On top of dealing with Mom's issues, Lori has held down a full-time job and raised a family. Fortunately, her family has been a great source of support. Emily and Andy make visits on their own to visit their grandma. And Paul has been so good to his mother-in-law. He usually accompanies Lori on her twice a week visits to Mom, and whenever a trip to the emergency room has been required. His playfulness towards Mom often elicits smiles and laughter.

Lori has been somewhat like my "teacher" whenever I come to visit Mom. She is so in tune with Mom's moods and reactions that she can give me helpful hints on how to relate to her. Like when I try to feed my mother and she purses her lips and shakes her head as if to say "No more."

"Just wait a few seconds and try again," Lori has advised. "She'll usually eat more." And she usually does.

Or like Lori's advice to Ray "Try kissing her hand. She seems to get a kick out of that whenever Paul does it." So Ray tries, and the hand-smooching routine has elicited shoulder shaking giggles.

But from my perspective, the thing I personally appreciate most is the way that Lori has always kept me informed about what is happening with Mom. Sometimes it gets so frustrating living far away and feeling so removed. I think Lori understands that and tries to keep me abreast of everything. Whether it's a call to tell about another one of Mom's "spells", or about something funny she did during a visit, or just to tell me that a beautician came in to cut Mom's hair, Lori has always made the effort to help me feel connected. I'm so grateful for that. I've often wished I could do more to ease some of Lori's stress.

Brenda

I guess that leads to what my role has been on this long road. Initially, in the early stages of Mom's Alzheimer's, I felt I was able to do more to help out. At least I could make trips home, bringing food along and/or cooking meals at Mom's to be frozen for future use. I could clean the house whenever I visited. I could bring Mom home with me from time to time. But once she went into assisted living, it was harder to know how to help out in any major way.

I've come to learn that as the "long-distant daughter" there's not really any grand thing I can do, but it's the small gestures than can make a difference. Just always being there on the other end of the phone line for my sister, I believe, has helped ease her stress. She knows that if she has had a bad day, I'm only a phone call away. There's not much I can do other than listen. But sometime just listening is enough.

Also, little things like providing Mom's supply of Depends was helpful. I always brought several packages whenever I came to see Mom and sent checks to Lori in between those visits. That was just one less thing that she had to think about.

My sister is a huge Green Bay Packer fan. So one time when they visited us, Ray and I took Lori and Paul on the Lambeau Stadium tour. Another time we surprised them with tickets to a Packer football game. It was only a preseason game, but my sister was thrilled!

But even trumping that football game was a simple card I sent her one Christmas. I included a note expressing my appreciation for all she does for Mom. It must have come at one of those times when she was feeling a lot of stress. She called me immediately. "That is the best Christmas gift I'll receive this year," she said, her voice breaking. "I'm going to save this card forever. It means so much just to know that I'm appreciated." I felt very close to her during that call.

In fact, Lori and I have grown much closer than we ever used to be. I mentioned previously how I would cherish weekly phone conversations with my mom. And Lori would see Mom almost every day. We each were close to Mom in our own way, but yet somewhat distant from each other. Since we have joined together in this battle against Alzheimer's, a week does not go by without one of us calling the other. We don't always talk about Mom, either. Sometimes it's about our families, The Green Bay Packers, and yes, even politics. I now talk to Lori in much the same way that I had carried on conversations with Mom.

I used to feel such a loss when I'd return to Michigan and Mom would not be there to run out and greet me with a hug like she used to. Now when I go to visit, I stay at Lori's house and *she's* the one to greet me with that hug. Last November Lori, Paul, Emily, and Andy all came to Wisconsin for a holiday get-together with my family. When it was time to leave, my "kid" sister and I embraced and she whispered to me "It's just you and me now kid." I knew exactly what she meant. For now, Lori and I are the only ones left of the Ken and Helen Geiger family to preserve precious memories of our past family life. There is no one else on this earth that has shared the same childhood experiences with me as we grew up side by side. The past and the present have merged into a feeling of closeness with my sister that may not have been possible, had not Mom's illness brought us closer together. Strong bonds of sisterhood and friendship have formed between us that will never be broken.

Lori and Brenda at the Feet of Vince Lombardi

Ray, Mike, Brenda, Lori, Paul at Lambeau Stadium

MOM TODAY

Due to declining health and diminishing finances, Mom was moved into a nursing home in July of 2010. It was almost five years to the day since she had moved into assisted living. Our prerequisite of a "homey" place (that we had established for choosing the first residence) no longer applied. Since Mom seemed unaware of her surroundings, furnishings and atmosphere weren't important anymore.

Admittedly, mom's newest home is more of an institutional type setting. However, it is a clean, welcoming, and basically cheerful place. Lori and I remain satisfied with our selection. We were fortunate that there was an opening in the Portage facility. Once again it is relatively close-by Lori's home, making it easier for her to visit.

I also continue to visit whenever I can. Mom rarely acknowledges me at all these days. Occasionally she will give me a look, widening her eyes, as if to say "Oh, it's you," but I'm lucky if I get that much. Obviously there is no verbal communication from her, other than garbled sounds as she might try to speak. Usually she just sits quietly, and I do as well. I hold her hand or stroke her arms, trying to a least communicate with the sense of touch. Sometimes I give her a scalp massage, lightly stroking her head with my fingertips. I think she likes this. Sometimes a moan of pleasure escapes from her.

Usually someone else will come along with me so we can quietly talk while spending time with Mom. My close friend, Marcia, will frequently stop by so we can catch up on one another's lives. Marcia has been so supportive throughout the years. We've been friends since high school and have shared many good and bad times together. It was during one such visit that I want to relate this amazing story.

It happened sometime around Christmas in 2009 (Mom was still at assisted living yet). Anyway, I was feeding her lunch, and Marcia and I were quietly chatting. My son, Mike, had also accompanied me on this visit, as he had on many numerous occasions. "Mom, can I feed Grandma?" he asked. I was touched that he would want to. Most young men his age want to stay as far away as possible from a nursing home, let alone feed someone. But Mike has always been soft-hearted and kind to the core. "Sure," I said, handing over the spoon. Mike began feeding her small spoonfuls of her meal, while Marcia and I continued to talk.

Suddenly all conversation stopped and the three of us looked at each other in amazement. "Did you hear that?" we all asked each other. We had to confirm that we weren't imagining what we all *knew* we had heard. Mom had clearly murmured "Mike". (It reminded me of the time when Mom had spoken my aunt's nickname "Itily May" though that had happened years earlier). Later, when I told Lori and her family about what happened, we all agreed we had been given a small Christmas miracle. At this point we'll take them in any size.

I think it is so important that people who live in nursing homes not be forgotten. I've continued to send cards on every holiday and have included my kids' names on those greetings. I should mention that those "kids" are now grown. Two are married and they all three have moved away. Anyway, this year I asked them if they would please send their grandma a Christmas card themselves. Of course they all readily agreed. I know that Mom doesn't know the difference. But others who care for her and come into her room will see the cards and have one more reminder that she isn't a lost, forgotten soul. On the same line of thinking, last Christmas I also purchased a gift to them from their grandma. Mom always was enchanted by angels and collected them through the years. I saw to it my children and their new spouses each received a ceramic angel from their Grandma Helen. It's what she would have given if she could.

I hope friends don't hesitate to ask me how my mom is doing, fearing it will make me sad. Actually the opposite is the case. Somehow it cheers me to know that others care, and that, once again, Mom is not forgotten. When my son, Dan, was married this past August, Ray stood up at Dan and Amy's reception to say a few words. He remembered my mom and dad along with Grandma and Grandpa Springhetti (who also couldn't celebrate with us at the wedding due to a health problem). My husband's words were touching. Just including them all in a small remembrance statement, made them present in our hearts.

So Mom lives a quiet, peaceful existence these days. She sleeps a lot and seems to be eating less, as evidenced by gradual weight loss. Sometimes I bake her favorite coconut macaroons and leave a small tin of them in her room. My hope is that her aids will occasionally take some time to feed her one as a special treat. I pray that Mom continues to have compassionate caregivers, and I wonder what they think of her. It saddens me that no one who has daily contact with her now, knows the Helen that we all knew and loved.

I recently came across a poem I had clipped from a publication years ago. I'm usually not one to clip articles, but this one touched me enough to cause me to save it. Ironically, as I read it now, it seems so relevant to my mom as well as others confined to nursing homes today. Maybe it's no accident that I saved it so long ago.

In researching this poem, I discovered it was written by a woman who died in the geriatric ward of Ashludie Hospital near Dunde, Scotland. It was found among her meager possessions and so impressed the staff that copies were made and distributed to every nurse in the hospital. (Another source credits one of her nurses as the person who actually wrote it and gave it to this lady). Regardless, since then it has been published in the Beacon House News of the Northern Ireland Mental Health Association and a Focus on the Family magazine where I first read it in 1985. It has gained world wide recognition through the internet and has two titles: "A Young Girl Still Dwells" and "See Me". This poem is a touching reminder to all of us to look closer to see the real person inside.

What do you see, nurse, what do you see?
Are you thinking when you look at me—
A crabbed old woman, not very wise,
Uncertain of habit with far away eyes,
Who dribbles her food and makes no reply
When you say in a loud voice—"I do wish you'd try."
Who seems not to notice the things that you do
And forever is losing a stocking or shoes,
Who resisting or not, lets you do as you will
With bathing and feeding, the long day to fill.
Is that what you're thinking, is that what you see?
Then open your eyes, nurse. You're not looking at me.

I'll tell you who I am as I sit here so still.
As I move at your bidding, eat at your will,
I'm a small child of ten with a father and mother,
Brothers and sisters who love one another:
A young girl of sixteen with wings on her feet,
Dreaming that soon a love she'll meet;
A bride at twenty, my heart gives a leap
Remembering the vows that I promised to keep;
At twenty-five now I have young of my own
Who need me to build a secure, happy home.

A woman of thirty, my young now grow fast,
Bound together with ties that should last.
At forty, my young sons have grown up and gone,
But my man's beside me to see I don't mourn.
At fifty once more babies play round my knee—
Again we know children, my loved one and me.
Dark days are upon me, my husband is dead.
I look to the future, I shudder with dread.
For my young are all rearing young of their own,
And I think of the years and the love that I've known.

I'm an old woman now and nature is cruel
'Tis her jest to make old age look like a fool.
The body it crumbles, grace and vigor depart.
There is a stone where I once had a heart.
But inside this old carcass, a young girl still dwells,
And now again my bittered heart swells.
I remember the joys, I remember the pain
And I'm loving and living life over again.
I think of the years, all too few, gone too fast,
And accept the stark fact that nothing can last.
So open your eyes, nurse, open and see
Not a crabbed old woman,
Look closer—see me!

Helen's Last Visit Home with her Family

Brenda and Beryl Returning Helen to Assisted Living Later That Day

Spending Quiet Moments in the Courtyard

FAITH, HOPE, AND UNEXPECTED BLESSINGS

As I sit at this computer today, trying to get my final thoughts down, I am amazed at how many memories over the past years came back to me. This process certainly has been an emotional experience for me. I have found myself laughing and crying as my fingers have tapped out these words on the keyboard. I'm sure if I had only kept that journal, there would be so much more to fill a larger book. But I think enough has been said to adequately portray my mom and the love that her family has for her. This disease has robbed her of so much, yet she still maintains a demeanor of quiet dignity and peaceful resignation. She has always had such a joy for life, a joy she has shared with others. The laughter that was so much a part of Mom still bubbles up occasionally, though usually it has been replaced by a slight smile.

It is important to note that this story of Mom's long battle with Alzheimer's could be retold by countless other families. Families, like ours, who struggle with a loved one, taking one step at a time along this dark, uncertain road. It is a road that has been filled with pot holes, ruts, and unpredictable twists and turns. But somehow we have all managed to navigate our way to this point that we find ourselves today. Although the journey has been hard, we have not been alone. There have been so many people who have provided support and help along the way.

Family and friends top the list, of course. But there have been others too. Like all the staff from adult day care, assisted living and the nursing home who have all given Mom compassionate care and given our family understanding throughout the years. Like the hospice worker who lent a listening ear to Lori, as well as assisting Mom with some needs. Like the doctor who assured us that we had made the right decision concerning a DNR issue. Like Mom's financial advisor who met with Lori and me every year to give us updates and solid advice. He always asked about Mom, and seemed truly concerned about her welfare.

Friends have also told me about the benefits of support groups for caregivers. Although Beryl and Lori never choose this route, it has been extremely helpful to others families. I would be lax not to mention organizations like The Alzheimer's Association, Alzheimer's Research, and others that continue to provide so much help and hope to families. These are only a few examples of many who have helped ease our way.

Besides the understandable sadness we have felt, there have also been times of laughter and unexpected blessings. The united relationship that evolved between Beryl, Lori, and me is one such blessing. And I have tried to describe some of the more amusing incidents that have left us all laughing.

Most important, is the feeling that a Guiding Hand has continued to lead our family, especially at crucial decision-making times. Once we decided to place Mom into an assisted living facility (and later a nursing home) the selection process seemed fairly easy. The director of the Home encouraged us to look at many places before making our choice, but advised us to ultimately "go with our gut feeling". Beryl, Lori, and I always seemed to unanimously have a strong sense that each particular place we chose felt right and we never regretted our decisions. Portage is a large, spread-out area. It amazes me when I think that all of the facilities that we liked the most were also all within a few miles of Mom's home! This made visiting so much easier for our family.

I think about Mom's unbelievable fast adjustment to her first new Home. Was my supervisor, Julie, right? Did our family pick just the right time to make that transition so easy? How did Lori and I know when we told Beryl "It's time" that it really *was* the exact right time?

And for that matter, what about the timing of the job I landed at an adult day care center not long before Mom, herself, was diagnosed with Alzheimer's? The knowledge I have gained from working with participants who also had this disease, certainly helped guide me into taking steps in Mom's behalf and helping her along this road. Were these all just coincidences? Or were they small miracles that made our journey easier? I believe the latter.

When I began writing this in honor of my mom, I decided on the title "The Long Road". But upon further reflection, I realize that a long road leading nowhere is an inadequate description of what our family (especially Mom) has been through. It is through our faith that we recognize that this road does, indeed, have a destination. It will eventually lead Mom (and all of us in our own time) to a new life with God and loved ones who have gone before.

I saw Mom again just last weekend. I didn't get much of a response from her—just a little smile a few times. She seemed sleepy and I wondered if she just preferred to be left alone to doze. When she's awake and seems so far away in her demeanor, I wonder what, if anything, she's thinking. Does she still have fleeting memories of her past? Does "a young girl still dwell" inside her, as the poem suggests?

I will continue to visit when I can, though I no longer feel an obligation keep to a certain time table. When I can't be with her physically, I try to stay close to her through prayer. I pray that God grants her a peaceful, pain-free existence (with perhaps a sense of joy still sprinkled in from time to time). I pray for continued compassionate caregivers to provide Mom that comfort care that is so important to her family. I pray for strength and endurance for Lori and me that we can continue to give her support in her final days. I pray for all these things with assurance, hope, and faith that this long road that Mom has traveled along for over twelve years now will eventually lead her Home.

THE END

Helen Geiger-Geren

Author's Note: Several weeks after the completion of this book, Mom peacefully passed away on April 6, 2011. Her memory lives on.